*My*
# PATH *to*
# TRUTH

SHIRLEY FERGUSON

WESTBOW
PRESS®
A DIVISION OF THOMAS NELSON
& ZONDERVAN

WestBow Press books may be ordered through
booksellers or by contacting:

WestBow Press
A Division of Thomas Nelson & Zondervan
1663 Liberty Drive
Bloomington, IN 47403
www.westbowpress.com
1 (866) 928-1240

ISBN: 978-1-5127-7184-8 (sc)
ISBN: 978-1-5127-7185-5 (e)

Library of Congress Control Number: 2017900609

Print information available on the last page.

WestBow Press rev. date: 01/19/2017

# Preface

This book is written purposely without names, in order to give the name of Jesus Christ glory and honor.

*"Neither is their salvation in any other; for there is none other name under heaven given among men, whereby we must be saved."*

-Acts 4:12

This book is dedicated to the Lord Jesus Christ, and to my husband and my children, and all their families.
Shirley Ferguson

*My Path To Truth* is the inspirational story of one woman's spiritual journey to find God. I feel honored that Sister Shirley Ferguson asked me to help prepare her manuscript for publication. My prayer is that others may find their path to salvation through this book.

Eloise Wampler—Gate City, VA

While reading *My Path To Truth,* it is evident that God not only had a special plan for Sister Ferguson's life, He also has one for you. Thank you for sharing your story.

Melissa Spears –Kingsport, TN

Sister Shirley has been a true blessing, opening her heart and home to me for over 35 years. We have shared so many memories together, both happy and sad. My most cherished memory was a visit with her just a few days after my Dad passed away. She met me at her door with open arms. I could feel the Spirit of the Lord as she stood there and held me. She handed me a piece of paper with the scripture written, Philippians 4:13. She asked me to claim it every morning and to keep it on my person at all times. I took her advice. Since that day, this scripture has become my favorite bible verse. It has given me what I have needed for almost eight years. I have shared this verse with so many people. Thank you, Shirley, for sharing this with me. Your acts of caring and sharing will never be forgotten.

Cindy Edwards—Bristol, TN

This is an inspirational story that will stir up your faith.

Peggy—Chicago, IL

This book is proof that if one hungers and thirsts after righteousness (*Matthew 5:6*), he shall be filled. Because of a thirst and hunger for God, and obedience of God's word, Sister Ferguson received what she needed from God. Her book stirs up a hunger for righteousness and is proof that if one hungers and thirsts, you will be filled.

Sister Sarah Chapman-Williams—Kingsport, TN

A very insightful and touching look into the familial and spiritual journey of a gracious and Godly woman. The truth of God's blessed grace given to undeserving people and His pursuit of every individual is truly heartening.

Jim Long—Blountville, TN

This book is the inspiring and sincere story of Shirley Ferguson's faith journey. She speaks from her heart about the trials and sufferings in her life and then reveals the redemptive power of Jesus Christ. She is a wonderful example of the power of God in one's personal life.

Hazel Salama—Kingsport, TN

A very enjoyable read. Anyone who reads it will surely be blessed.

Betsy Waldrep—Bowling Green, KY

# Contents

# Spiritual Beginnings

The casket sat in the corner of the living room in southwest Virginia. The whole family gathered close by. Friends and neighbors filled the room and overflowed into the yard and other parts of the house. I was standing near the door to the front porch, a girl of about thirteen years, watching and listening to what was happening. Three women were standing on the left side of the casket, and they began to sing, "He lives, He lives, Christ Jesus lives today … You ask me how I know He lives? He lives within my heart."

The words became part of me. They went straight into my heart. I sang them over and over and over.

The funeral was finished. Now we were on our way to the graveyard, which was located about one and a half miles from our house. My dad's loving aunt, who had lived in Florida, was being laid to rest. The family visited for a while and then departed. Many had traveled from Florida and North Carolina and had to journey home. Oh, what a sad and mournful time. Now they were gone, but the song, "He Lives" was embedded in my heart.

# Our Church

Our family lived in the country about two miles from town. The little white church was located at the top of the hill, right off the tar road. We walked to church. Every Sunday morning we could hear the church bell ringing. Sometimes we could hear the piano playing and a woman singing the beautiful old-time hymns, such as "At the Cross" and "Power in the Blood." There were no microphones in those days, but the church door was open, and the music and words floated out to greet us as we and others walked up the hill.

This was the church of my childhood, and I loved it. We were taught the catechism. Every year we had Bible school. I still have my certificates today. We always had a Christmas play, and I usually played the part of an angel. They always gave everyone a treat bag of oranges, candy, and nuts. In the summertime, we had a picnic. I can still remember the good sandwiches and the fun we had.

Our church was a big room. The presbyter came once a month, but on other Sundays, a local landowner taught the lesson. The whole church family sang together and then went to the sections marked off in the corners for each Sunday school class. We all came together again for prayer, singing, announcements, and the dismissal. The church was a holy place, and we were taught to have respect for the sanctuary. I loved the Lord, and I felt loved by the church.

As I grew, I started reading the Bible. I studied and read Acts 2:38–39. *"Then Peter said unto them, Repent, and be baptized every one of you in the name of Jesus Christ for the remission of sins, and ye shall receive the gift of the Holy Ghost. For the promise is unto you and to your children, and to all that are afar off, even as many as the Lord our God shall call." I* asked the church teacher about it and was told that this was for the church back then. He said this verse did not apply to us today, because the Old Testament was for them, and we had the New Testament. He was a man of authority, and I believed him. The Lord was drawing me by His Spirit, and when I was sixteen years old, I repented during a revival and was sprinkled. I was saved.

# The Sufferings of Others

One of my friends who sometimes walked to church with me was killed in an auto accident while visiting relatives in another state. She was a senior, and I was a junior in high school. We were at a ball game when this heartbreaking news was announced. She was buried in her prom dress. Everyone in the school mourned.

One of my sister's close friends died at sixteen. She had rheumatic heart disease. Pain, suffering, and sorrow—it seemed that was all there was.

# Preparation

I wanted to be a missionary. I wanted to help people. There were no programs to become a missionary, so, at the beginning of the ninth grade, I took the pre-entrance exam to enter nursing school. I took all the required courses, and when I graduated from high school, I was accepted into the local school of nursing. I was seventeen years old. My dad paid the required amount of money and bought everything on the list of things I needed.

I lived in the nurse's dorm, attended classes, and worked in the hospital for my training and my room and board. After six months, I was capped in the big church on Main Street and given my Florence of Nightingale lamp light. I took the oath of a nurse. For two years I worked and studied. Money was scarce and hard to come by.

It was at this time also, that I gave in to peer pressure and started smoking. I wanted to be included. I became addicted to cigarettes and would need God to deliver me from them. I went home as often as I could. The people from my church always asked about me, and I saw them from time to time.

Seven of us nursing students were sent to Maryland to study psychiatry. We traveled by train and had many trunks filled with our belongings. This was the first time I had been so far away from home. We trained at the hospital in Maryland for three months before returning home.

About that time, I quit the local school of nursing because of a romantic relationship that had gone sour. I was hired to work in the psychiatric hospital where I had just trained. I lived in the nurses' residence on the hospital grounds. I inquired about the Maryland State Board exams and attended the University of Maryland to meet the state requirements. I took the state boards and passed.

I got another job at the hospital in the city. I moved into the YWCA. I had a small room, and walked to the stop and then rode the trolley to work. I ate most of my meals at the hospital or nearby restaurants. In the summer it was very hot and humid. There was no air conditioning in the hospital where I worked. My starched white uniform was always very wrinkled by lunch time.

I made several good friends from other countries, but I got homesick at times. I traveled home on the Greyhound bus when I had enough time off from work, which was not often. My dad came to visit me once when I got very homesick. My mother and I wrote letters to one another regularly, and she kept me informed about the family.

As a nurse in the city hospital, I observed many evil happenings, and I began to wonder, "If the Lord is in us all, how can these things happen?" For example, a young man was shot around midnight. He was brought to the hospital. They operated and removed the bullet. ICU, the unit where I worked, received all the patients from surgery. It was my duty to monitor his vital signs. About five a.m., he slipped off into eternity. There was nothing I could do. In another case, a drunken man tied his wife to their bed and set the bed on fire. She was rescued from the flames, and he was taken to jail. She cried in agony, and it took months for her to heal. She had a badly scarred face and body, but she was alive. I could not understand how anyone could be so cruel and mean.

# Confusion and Hope

For the first time in my life, I was exposed to other beliefs, such as the beliefs of Catholics, Episcopalians, and Lutherans. I heard about purgatory, which my dictionary defined as a region between heaven and hell. I wondered which religion was the right one. I began to wonder if I was really saved and hoped that I would go to heaven if I died.

To work and back was my everyday routine. I wondered if this was what my life was going to be. I hoped and prayed for something good to happen to me. I hoped that the Lord loved me and heard my prayers. At Christmastime, the Salvation Army rang the bells. The bells told the story, a time for gifts and giving, the birth of the Savior. I always gave something to the bell ringers and was glad I could. I would not be giving or receiving any gifts this year. I would be working. I would give myself to those I cared for. That was all I had to give.

# Happiness

One day I met a special someone. We worked together, and soon we were married. We moved to New Jersey to give him the opportunity to specialize in his vocation. A son was born to us, and we were overjoyed at his birth. Everything was normal until about two weeks after his birth; then he began to projectile vomit.

He could not keep his formula down. After each feeding, he would vomit. He was a small baby and was losing weight rapidly. We were so worried. We made several visits to the pediatrician's office, changed his formula, and tried a few other things. Then, the pediatrician decided to X-ray our son's stomach. I called my brother to come because I knew that if something was not done, he would die. The X-ray showed that my baby had congenital pyloristenosis, meaning the opening between his stomach and the small intestine was abnormally narrow. Surgery was performed, and then he could eat and retain his food.

By the time my brother and his wife arrived, we had wonderful news to tell them, thank God. Soon after this, I visited my parents in Virginia. While I was there, I borrowed my brother-in-law's car, and my sister took me to get my driver's license. When I became pregnant with my daughter, Rh-negative antibodies were discovered in my type-O blood. I was told that I would have to take caution for the baby. In my seventh month, I went into labor, and after twenty-five hours, my little girl was born. She was very jaundiced. She spent ten days in an incubator, and then we took her home. After we fed her every three hours for one month and gave her special care, she began to show signs that she was going to make it. Again, we were so thankful to God.

During this time we saved our money, and when my husband had finished his specialized training, we traveled to Egypt, the country of my husband. He was of the Coptic Orthodox Christian faith. In the Coptic Church in Cairo, Egypt, the priest baptized my son and daughter. It is their custom that the children are the faith of their father.

The Egyptian people were all so loving and kind, but I missed my country and family. I wrote two poems while there, out of loneliness for my family and for America.

After two and a half years, we returned to America, settling in Michigan. Many of our neighbors were of the Catholic and Lutheran religions. We made friends quickly. My husband had a good job, and after a few years we were able to buy a house. All the neighborhood children played in our yard, and we were happy. Each year I eagerly awaited spring break so we could visit my family in Virginia.

# Longing

You are all here with me, because
you are all here in my heart.
I hear no word from you
yet we are not apart.
My heart is sad, but my eyes are clear.
For the light of your love guides me
As if you were near.
I hear your voices long in memory, yet
I see you not.
I can remember what we said and did.
It's all that I have got.
With my eyes I see a foreign land.
With palm trees and sand.
I hear a language I do not know.
I live on unweary, for the time
is almost gone. A few more months,
And I shall be home.

# America, Southwest Virginia

There is a land far away,
Where the people all speak in a funny way.
Some call them hillbillies, some call them poor.
But these people are very much more.
They are good-hearted, gentle and kind,
And nowhere on earth can you find
A country like mine.
Hills and gardens to brighten your view,
Whippoorwills calling, birds singing to you.
Oh! How I remember the pleasures I had,
When I was a girl, and was with my dad.
Picking berries, hoeing corn.
What a wonderful feeling to have been born
In all of this beauty, that no one can see,
No one except the hillbillies and me.

# Sickness and Sorrow

On one occasion, the children and I were traveling on a Greyhound bus, going to visit my parents. As usual, we were very excited about the trip. The children loved being with their grandparents, aunts, uncles, and cousins. As the bus was pulling out and we were waving good-bye to my husband, I noticed that he did not look well. His face had an ashen color. As the bus rolled south, taking me farther and farther from him, I became more and more worried.

When we arrived at our destination, my family was waiting for us. They had received a telephone call for us to return home quickly. My husband had suffered a massive heart attack. He was still alive, but they did not expect him to live. My brother, who had been waiting for us at the bus station, took us to my parent's house. We made arrangements to fly immediately back to Michigan.

My husband lived, but his heart was so damaged that he was not a candidate for heart surgery. He had to be treated medically. After gaining enough strength to be released from the hospital, he was put on a very strict diet and special exercise with limited activity.

Soon after he was released from the hospital, I became very ill with a high fever. The doctors could not determine the cause. I was admitted to the hospital in a delirious state. They ran tests, and thought that I may have been bitten by a tick when I was in the south a few weeks earlier. I was put on bed rest, and broke out in large hives all over my body from the medication I was taking. I was afraid for my life. The Lord spoke to me and told me that if the palms of my hands and the soles of my feet did not get hives, then I would live. I looked often, and when no hives appeared in those two places, I knew I was going to live.

There was a woman in the bed next to me, and several people came into the room and prayed with her. They asked me if they could pray for me, and I gladly said, "Yes." This was the first time in my life that I had seen prayer with laying of hands on a sick person. I got better and went home. A loving person had flown from Raleigh, North Carolina, to care for my husband and children, and she cared for me also, until I regained my strength. The cause of my illness remains unknown and I was never diagnosed.

I believe now, and did then, that it was by divine appointment that I was in the hospital at the time to be prayed for.

The doctor had told my husband to stop smoking. He tried and I tried, but we were both unsuccessful. I began to worry what God thought about smoking. I read in the

King James Version of the Bible about defiling the temple. *"Know ye not that ye are the temple of God, and that the Spirit of God dwelleth in you? If any man defile the temple of God, him shall God destroy; for the temple of God is holy, which ye are."* (1 Corinthians. 3:16-17) I began to feel very bad that I smoked, but I was so addicted to nicotine that I could not stop. The more I tried to quit, the more I smoked.

My husband regained his health, enough to go back to work and drive a car again. Life became normal. One night we were at a dinner party, and I overheard a woman tell another woman that you had to be baptized to be saved. I did not sleep all that night. I had not been baptized. I had been sprinkled. I began to question the salvation I had taken for granted.

Time passed. Life was good. Everything was going the way it should. We were happy. Then my husband became sick again. He had to be hospitalized with bleeding ulcers. Soon after that, he had another heart attack. Diet, exercise, rest, and medication, and he was soon back to work. He had relatives in nearby Ohio, and they came to visit us often. We attended the Coptic Orthodox church together for mass. His father, mother, and sister came to America for a month-long visit. We had a wonderful time being together again and visiting others.

The years passed. My husband was able to work, but physically weak. He opened his own office and struggled to meet the demands on his time. I prayed and asked God to let him live, at least until the children grew up. I began to read in John, Chapter 3 about being born again:

*"Jesus answered and said unto him, Verily, verily, I say unto thee, Except a man be born again, he cannot see the kingdom of God. Nicodemus saith unto him, How can a man be born when he is old? Can he enter the second time into his mother's womb, and be born? Jesus answered, Verily, verily, I say unto thee, Except a man be born of water and of the Spirit, he cannot enter into the kingdom of God. That which is born of the flesh is flesh; and that which is born of the Spirit is spirit. Marvel not that I said unto thee, Ye must be born again. The wind bloweth where it listedth, and thou hearest the sound thereof, but canst not tell whence it cometh, and whither it goeth; so is every one that is born of the Spirit. Nicodemus answered and said unto him, How can these thing be?" (John 3:3-9)*

I was just like Nicodemus; I sure did not know how to be born again. I began to ask God, just like Nicodemus did, "How can these things be?" My husband and I both loved to read. He was always reading the best sellers. We made regular trips to the library; I was drawn to the religious section. I would tell myself that the next time we came to the library, I would check out something non-religious. But when the time came, I always went back to the same section. I read the Psalms for comfort, and believed that God was with us and was taking care of us. I read John, Chapter 14, over and over, *"Let not your heart be troubled ..."* I had a troubled heart.

In those days, we had a lot of clothes that had to be ironed. Once a week I faced this large basket of work. I began to talk to God as I ironed. I spoke to Him out loud, and

I raised my hands to praise Him. I wept many times. I needed the reassurance of the Lord every day. I asked Him to ride with me in the car, and I talked to Him as I drove. I could not see Him, but I believed that He was there and was listening. I invited Him to sit at the table beside of me when I was alone.

My husband suffered two more heart attacks; he also had bleeding ulcers and was enduring much pain and suffering. The doctors told me over and over that he could go at any time. I asked the Lord not to let him die in the car, going to and from work. I prayed this every day and waited for him to return home safely in the evenings. We talked about his death and tried to make plans for the children and me after he was gone.

He knew that time was nearing, and he spent a lot of time with the children, trying to prepare them. We all took a plane trip together to visit my family. They loved him. It was his last visit.

We hoped and prayed that he would recover, but in January, following his fifth heart attack, he was gone. Congestive heart failure had won. The children and I were devastated. It was almost more than we could bear. All the friends, neighbors, and co-workers who had prayed and been with us through the years were there. After a Coptic Orthodox funeral, his body was flown to Virginia for a graveside service in the little graveyard located not far from my childhood home. The Presbyterian minister preached his funeral on a cold and frozen January day.

Brokenhearted, we returned to our home in Michigan. The children had to go to school. They had many young friends, and everyone tried to help in our sorrow. We could hardly face the days. I tried to take good care of the children and get things in order, paying off bills and bringing closure. I put our house up for sale, but it would not be available until the school year ended. One week before spring break, the house sold. I had prayed that the Lord would send a buyer, because I could not buy another house until our house sold.

During spring break we traveled to Virginia for a visit and to look for a house to buy. My dad and mom and especially one sister and others drove us to the real estate appointments. I liked one house in Virginia, but it sold before I could purchase it. There was nothing I was interested in near my parents. The only house available to us was in Tennessee. My father and brothers inspected it for quality, and my mom tried to be there for the children. The house was purchased with the understanding that we would move in June when the children got out of school. I felt that we were not alone and that the Lord was helping us.

We returned home and a well-known evangelist made preparations to come to our area. I was asked to help in the crusade. I did and was happy to do so. The message was "Jesus is The Bridge." My children, along with hundreds of others, went to the altar. Afterward, they received literature from this organization.

Also, the Orthodox Pope came to Detroit, and I attended the banquet given in his honor.

In the meantime, we were preparing our move to Tennessee. Our neighbors gave me a going-away party, and they gave me a plaque that read, "Bloom where you are planted." I felt I was hardly existing, let alone blooming. Another close family gave the children a going-away party to say good-bye to all their friends. In June when school was out, we moved. My brother and sister-in-law drove a large rental truck to help us. We packed and left early one morning. I drove my car with the children and followed the truck. As we were unpacking the truck, another sister-in-law gave birth to a precious baby boy. I had jokingly told her on the phone not to have the baby until we arrived.

The children and I spent most of our time at my parent's home. Several years before, my dad had suffered a heart attack, and he had emphysema, caused by cigarette smoking. He was sick now, and all my emotions, and energy went into helping him. It was good just to be with my parents, cooking, cleaning, and talking. My mother spent the evenings sewing quilt squares by hand, and I started sewing with her. When school started in the fall, the children made excellent grades and were very mature for their ages. I was very proud of them.

Sometimes when my dad was able, he and my mother drove to my house and spent the day with us. Dad would try to visit all his children in one day. My brother and sister and their families visited and helped us to cope. I loved to play with the new baby. Even now, as I write this, it is very hard to think of that time, but I feel it must be told.

# New Beginning

Time passed and I met another special person. I had thought that I would never marry again. The future, stretching out before me, looked bleak. We decided to get married. I was glad. About three months after we were married, I became pregnant. We were all so happy. About this time, my new father-in-law died suddenly. I was just getting to know him and was very sad about his death.

I went for my first check-up and the doctor told me not to have the baby. This was because of my age and the Rh factor. He would not take me as a patient, but referred me to another doctor in Winston Salem, North Carolina. I asked the Lord to let me have this baby. I would give him back to the Lord. I named my baby son that day.

My husband drove me to Winston Salem for all the prenatal care visits. We had to get up at 3:30 a.m. to be the first patient at 7:30 a.m. They would do all the tests, and then we would have to wait for the test results. It was usually after lunch before we could leave. I was given an experimental drug to help the baby. It made my hands, legs, and feet swell. I had to sign a form that I would not drive a car while taking the medicine. In the lobby of the hospital was a sign that read, "We minister to the body, soul, and spirit." I was glad, because I needed all three. Everyone at the hospital was so good to us.

My new husband had a wonderful family close by. I had the support of my family and we all eagerly awaited the birth of our child. The doctor waited until the baby's lungs were developed, and then in the eighth month he was delivered by C-section. He was a tiny little boy, and our hearts were filled with joy at his birth. In a few hours, we were told that they would have to take the baby to another hospital. My husband followed the ambulance and stayed with him while they did a blood exchange on him. Twenty-four hours later, they had to do another one. I was discharged from the hospital so I could visit my baby. We stayed in a Holiday Inn near the hospital. After one week, we were allowed to take him home.

My children had taken good care of themselves and our home. They loved their little brother. Thank you, Lord, for letting him live. I was so happy and glad. Then, suddenly he was anemic. He had to go to the hospital for a blood transfusion. My heart was filled with fear. *"Let not your heart be troubled ..."* (John 14:1) I tried to believe everything would be all right.

The baby did fine for a while, then one morning, he stopped breathing. He was beginning to turn blue. I grabbed him and ran to the bathroom where it was warm, rubbing him all over as I went. He started breathing again. My daughter and I took him to the hospital where they did tests and observed his breathing for several days. He was discharged with orders to have a monitor placed in his crib. An alarm would go off if his breathing stopped. At the end of one year, we were able to remove the monitor.

Our little boy grew and brought much happiness to us all. He was a special gift from God; and he was so loved by everyone.

# Salvation

The Lord was dealing with me, drawing me by His Spirit. Every time I heard the theme song, "Just a Man", before a preaching message on television, I would quickly run to listen to it. I also began to listen to gospel tapes. I took my little son and went to a gospel singing. I bought a tape and loved to hear it again and again. I got a magazine in the mail, which had an article about speaking in a heavenly language. I read it over and over, and I began to pray that I would speak in a heavenly language. A tent revival was set up not far from our home. I wanted to go, so my husband, son, and I went. I had never been in a service like that. People were shouting, praying, and worshipping the Lord. The minister called for a prayer line and for all the other ministers to come up on the platform. I was very interested in this, for it was all new to me.

My daughter was attending a local church on Sunday mornings. When she was asked if she would like to be baptized, she came to me for advice. I did not know what to tell her, so I said, "You will just have to decide whether or not to be baptized."

On Easter Sunday I wanted to go to the sunrise service. My daughter and I went together. It was raining, and the service was held inside. The people were very nice, and they dedicated a song to me, but when the service was over I felt disappointed. The same day, I dressed my little son in a three-piece suit I had made for him to wear on Easter, and we went to another church. After that service, I felt so disappointed. I told the Lord, "Twice I have gone out to meet you today, and you did not come."

My older children graduated from high school with honors and went away to college. I was still searching for something from God. One day I noticed an advertisement in the paper about a revival in a church downtown. My sister-in-law and I discussed it, and we both wanted to go. We had never attended this church, and we knew no one there. Her family of four and my husband, son and I attended the service. People were praying out loud, shouting, and weeping. They also raised their hands in worship. I had not seen this kind of service before. I also felt the presence of God and I felt reverence for the house of God. I was so glad I was there.

My sister-in-law and her family were also enjoying the presence of God. They were all baptized that first night of revival. We went back to several more revival services. I was asked to attend a class for women on Tuesday nights. I went to the class, and I loved it. I had noticed the first night that most of the women had beautiful, long hair. I was eager to find out more about this new way of living for God.

My father had been sick for many years, and his health was failing rapidly. Suddenly, in early June, he left us. The grief was more than I could bear. I realized that my heart was cracked when my husband died, but now it was broken. I felt I could not go on. I found comfort in Isaiah 61:1 and Luke 4:18.

*"The Spirit of the Lord God is upon me; because the LORD hath anointed me to preach good tidings unto the meek; he hath sent me to bind up the brokenhearted, to proclaim liberty to the captives, and the opening of the prison to them that are bound;"* (Isaiah 61:1)

*"The Spirit of the Lord is upon me, because he hath anointed me to preach the gospel to the poor; he hath sent me to heal the brokenhearted, to preach deliverance to the captives, and recovering of sight to the blind, to set at liberty them that are bruised,"* (Luke 4:18)

In July, I attended the church on a Wednesday. The pastor was preaching about being baptized. I wanted to stand up and shout, "Baptize me!" Suddenly, I had a pain in my chest, so I sat still until it went away. He continued preaching, and then again he said, "You must be baptized." I wanted to stand up and shout like before, "Baptize me!" Again, the pain came so severe I thought I was having a heart attack. I got up and went to the restroom. After a few minutes, the pain left. After the service, I talked to the pastor and told him that I wanted to be baptized. I told him about the pain I had experienced while he was preaching. He explained that the enemy of my soul had caused that to keep me from being baptized. I told the pastor that I smoked, and I needed God to help me stop. I said, "I know me. I will be baptized and then go right to my car and smoke. I don't want to be a hypocrite." The pastor said, "You do your part, and God will do His part." I believed him and trusted God to do his part.

We made plans for me to be baptized on the following Sunday after the service. The church was in revival, and a minister from another state was teaching on prayer. I was so excited. I had invited all of my family to witness the memorable occasion. The church was full. People were shouting and praising God. The pastor came to me and told me he felt led of God to baptize me right then and not to wait until after the service. I agreed and followed him upstairs. I changed into a baptismal robe. The visiting minister put me down into the water to be baptized in the name of Jesus Christ for the remission of my sins. I had a vision. I was standing behind a pulpit preaching in a foreign language. I was waving my hands and preaching to about 3,000 people. There was a sensation like Morse code on my forehead. I understand in English what I was preaching to the people. "It is real. It is true. His truth endureth forever." I looked down and wondered where I was, and suddenly it came gushing up out of my belly and I was shouting in an unknown tongue!

I was so happy! I hugged everyone. For about an hour I hardly knew where I was. Then at the end of service, I was asked to testify. I took the microphone and told about the vision I had. I had received the baptism of the Holy Ghost, speaking in tongues as evidence. I understood finally, at last. All my questions were answered. I was a sinner and had been spiritually blind. The Lord had opened my blinded eyes.

*"And I will bring the blind by a way that they knew not; I will lead them in paths that they have not known: I will make darkness light before them, and crooked things straight. These things will I do unto them, and not forsake them."* (Isaiah 42:16)

*"Therefore if any man be in Christ, he is a new creature: old things are passed away; behold, all things are become new."* (2 Corinthians 5:17)

My heart was filled with joy and gladness. I shouted, "Hallelujah, hallelujah to God, the Redeemer of my soul." I thanked Him for caring about me as an individual and for saving me, an unworthy sinner. That is why He came and died. He paid the debt and set me free. I have been born of His Spirit, washed by His blood!

I did my part, as the pastor had said, and God did His part. I have never smoked another cigarette. I can see how God has always been with me, all my life, and He has been drawing me closer and closer to Him. This has been my path to truth. I hope you will reflect on your path, and allow God to lead you into the fullness of the truth.

# Adding to the Foundation

For a long time, I had a burning desire to go to Bible College. The Lord made a way for me to graduate from the Untied Christian Bible Institute of Cleveland, Tennessee, becoming a licensed and ordained minister.

Many years have passed since I was baptized in Jesus name and received the gift of the Holy Ghost. I have been through many trials, but the Lord has delivered me through each one. I never smoked another cigarette after the Lord delivered me and that has been 29 years. *"If the Son therefore shall make you free, ye shall be free indeed."* (John 8:36)

The promises of God are real, but we as individuals have to activate them in our lives. We must meditate on them (eat the word) and get it in our hearts. Next, we must speak the Word and do it.

His Word will not return void. Isaiah 55:11 tells us, *"So shall my word be that goeth forth out of my mouth: it shall not return unto me void, but it shall accomplish that which I please, and it shall prosper in the thing whereto I sent it."*

# The Plan of Salvation

*"Then Peter said unto them, Repent, and be baptized every one of you in the name of Jesus Christ for the remission of sins, and ye shall receive the gift of the Holy Ghost. For the promise is unto you and to your children, and to all that are afar off, even as many as the Lord our God shall call."*

(Acts 2:38-39)

*"Wherefore God also hath highly exalted him, and given him a name which his above every name: That at the name of Jesus every knee should bow, of things in heaven, and thing in earth, and things under the earth; And that every tongue should confess that Jesus Christ is Lord, to the glory of God the Father."*

(Philippians 2:9-11)

The following are a few scriptures about the Word:

**It is the Word of life.** *"Holding forth the word of life; that I may rejoice in the day of Christ, that I have not run in vain, neither labored in vain."* (Philippians 2:16)

**The Word is living and active.** *"For the word of God is quick, and powerful, and sharper than any twoedged sword,* piercing even unto the dividing asunder of soul and spirit, and of the joints and marrow, and is a discerner of the thoughts and intents of the heart." (Hebrews 4:12)

**The Word of God is sure.** *"The works of his hands are verity and judgement; all his commandments are sure. They stand fast for ever and ever, and are done in truth and uprightness."* (Psalm 111:7-8)

**The Word of God is truth.** *"Thy righteousness is an everlasting righteousness, and thy law is the truth."* (Psalm 119:142)

**The Word is to be spoken.** *"The prophet that hath a dream, let him tell a dream; and he that hath my word, let him speak my word faithfully …"* (Jeremiah 23:28)

**God's Word is pure.** *"Every word of God is pure; he is a shield unto them that put their trust in him."* (Proverbs 30:5)

**His name is the Word of God.** *"And he was clothed with a vesture dipped in blood: and his name is called the Word of God."* (Revelation 19:13)

**The Word is God.** *"In the beginning was the Word, and the Word was with God, and the Word was God."* (John 1:1)

*\*Scriptures from Thompson Chain Reference Study Bible.*

Printed in the United States
By Bookmasters

Printed in the United States
By Bookmasters

WESTBOW
PRESS'
A DIVISION OF THOMAS NELSON
& ZONDERVAN

SHIRLEY FERGUSON

UNSEEN *Angels* HEAVENLY ENCOUNTERS

Scripture quotations are taken from the King James Version of the Bible.

WestBow Press books may be ordered through
booksellers or by contacting:

WestBow Press
A Division of Thomas Nelson & Zondervan
1663 Liberty Drive
Bloomington, IN 47403
www.westbowpress.com
1 (866) 928-1240

ISBN: 978-1-5127-7184-8 (sc)
ISBN: 978-1-5127-7185-5 (e)

Library of Congress Control Number: 2017900609

Print information available on the last page.

WestBow Press rev. date: 01/19/2017

*Are they not all ministering spirits, sent forth to minister for them who shall be heirs of salvation?*
*Hebrews 1:14 (King James Version)*

By Shirley Ferguson

*Seek ye the LORD while he may be found,*
*call ye upon him while he is near:*
*Isaiah 55:6*

The purpose of this book is to encourage others to know Jesus Christ and develop a daily relationship with Him.

Dedicated to:
My husband and helper, my precious children
and their spouses, whom I treasure, my darling
grandchildren, and my beloved great granddaughter.

# Contents

# Contents

# Born Again

On July 29, 1984, I was baptized in the name of Jesus Christ. The church was in revival, and a minister from another state was teaching on prayer. The church was full of people, shouting and praising God. The visiting minister put me down into the water to be baptized in the name of Jesus Christ for the remission of my sins. I had a vision, which began with me standing behind a pulpit preaching in a foreign language. I was waving my hands and preaching to about three thousand people. Then there was a sensation like Morse code on my forehead with the understanding in English that I was saying to the people, "It is real. It is true. His truth endureth forever." I looked down and wondered where I was, and suddenly, it came gushing out of my belly and I was shouting in an unknown tongue. I had been filled with the Holy Ghost, just like others in the Bible (Acts 8:12-17, Acts 10:44-17, Acts 11:15-17, Acts 19:1-6).

I smoked cigarettes for many years and was delivered that night. I never smoked another cigarette.

*Acts 2:38*
*Then Peter said unto them, Repent, and be baptized every one of you in the name of Jesus Christ for the remission of sins, and ye shall receive the gift of the Holy Ghost.*

*Acts 2:39*
*For the promise is unto you, and to your children, and to all that are afar off, even as many as the LORD our God shall call.*

# The Mantle

In church one Sunday morning, approximately 1985, we were worshiping God with hands raised and praising Him with our mouth when I looked up at the ceiling and a piece of material came floating down and fell on my head, stopping just above my shoulders. It was a mantle, grey in color. I went into the spirit. I don't know whose mantle I wear. No one else saw it, and I could not touch it; I was seeing in the spirit. Nevertheless, it was there.

A mantle is a garment. American Heritage dictionary describes a mantle as a loose sleeveless coat worn over outer garments; a cloak. Another meaning is something that covers, envelops, or conceals.

II Kings 2 tells us of a Biblical example of a mantle.

*8 And Elijah took his mantle, and wrapped it together, and smote the waters, and they were divided hither and thither, so that they two went over on dry ground.*

*12 And Elisha saw it, and he cried, My father, my father, the chariot of Israel, and the horsemen thereof. And he saw him no more: and he took hold of his own clothes, and rent them in two pieces.*

*13 He took up also the mantle of Elijah that fell from him, and went back, and stood by the bank of Jordan;*

*14 And he took the mantle of Elijah that fell from him, and smote the waters, and said, Where is the LORD God of Elijah? and when he also had smitten the waters, they parted hither and thither: and Elisha went over.*

# Old Bread

Many years ago after a Sunday morning service when I was attending a different church, I was feeling very down and did not know why. I had listened to the preaching and taken notes. It was very good. I had gone to church alone that morning and while leaving the church foyer, I asked God what made me feel so bad. As I walked to my car, just when I put my key to open the door, the Lord spoke two words to me, "Old bread." I understood immediately that the beautiful sermon I had heard was old, having no life in it. Fresh bread is prepared daily.

Christ is the bread of life. John 6:32-35

*32 Then Jesus said unto them, Verily, verily, I say unto you, Moses gave you not that bread from heaven; but my Father giveth you the true bread from heaven.*

*33 For the bread of God is he which cometh down from heaven, and giveth life unto the world.*

*34 Then said they unto him, Lord, evermore give us this bread.*

*35 And Jesus said unto them, I am the bread of life: he that cometh to me shall never hunger; and he that believeth on me shall never thirst.*

*Cast thy bread upon the waters: for thou*
*shalt find it after many days.*
*Ecclesiastes 11:1*

# Two Men or Were They Angels?

Many years ago when my youngest son was an infant, we rode with my husband to an Auto Parts store in Bristol, VA. We stayed in the car while my husband went inside to purchase the needed item.

I became aware that there was a car parked near me, full of women and their car would not start. I had compassion as I watched them trying to start the car. When my husband came out of the store, I asked him to help them for me. He asked if he could help them and they said, "Yes." In a short time, they were waving goodbye and thanking him for his help.

When my son was about 13 years old, I took him to a youth meeting at the church and I went to the mall to check out a vacuum cleaner on sale. When I came out of the store, my car would not start. Immediately, a black pickup truck pulled up beside me and the men inside asked if they could help. I gladly said, "Yes." They boosted the battery and I thanked them and drove to the exit of the parking lot. The car died once more. They were right there again and boosted the battery a second time.

I drove to the church and home without any problem. I was thankful they were there to help me that night. I remembered the women and their car that would not start all those years ago.

# Mary Sue, (The Angel)?

I had told the Lord I would do what he wanted me to do and go where he wanted me to go. I believe the following story was the Lord testing me to see if I really meant what I said.

One Sunday afternoon many years ago, I was alone and was resting in bed. I felt the Lord speak to me, telling me to go to Walmart in Bristol, TN.

I immediately got up and dressed and drove there on high alert. I went into the store and looked around, but bought nothing. I thought, well, I missed it. I came out of the store and there was a woman standing close to the exit. She spoke to me and asked me to take her home. I asked her why and she said it was too far for her to walk. I looked at her legs and they were covered with varicose veins. I had compassion on her; they were so bad. She told me the name of the street where she lived.

I was not familiar with it, but told her to get in the car and show me the way. She got in the car and asked me if I would buy her some candy at another store nearby. I drove there and asked her how much money she wanted. I gave it to her and she went into the store.

I was a little afraid. This was so weird. When she came back and got in the car with the candy, I told her the reason I hesitated to take her home was that I was afraid. She laughed and said she would not hurt anyone. She directed me to where she lived and I drove her there. As we were riding, I asked her what her name was and she said, "Mary Sue." I told her that I had a sister who lived in Florida named Mary Sue. When we arrived at the destination, she pointed to a building and said that was where she was going and she would walk the rest of the way. I let her out and she thanked me. I backed out of the driveway and turned to wave at her, but there was no one there. I never saw her again, and she did not have time to walk up the long driveway.

*Hebrews 13:2*
*Be not forgetful to entertain strangers: for thereby some have entertained angels unawares.*

*For God so loved the world, that he gave his only
begotten Son, that whosoever believeth in him
should not perish, but have everlasting life.
John 3:16*

# Thanksgiving Turkey

My husband and I had a routine of going to the nursing home each evening to care for my mother's needs. On this particular day before Thanksgiving one year, I was alone when I left the nursing home and went shopping at the local grocery store. I was feeling really down and unloved. I talked to the Lord as I pushed my buggy around the store. As I was leaving, I noticed that there was a box to register to win a Thanksgiving turkey. I said to the Lord, "If you are hearing me and if you love me, let me win this turkey." A few days later, there was a message on our answering machine that I had won the turkey.

# Christmas Turkey

One evening before going to the nursing home to visit my mother, I began thinking about how much she loved butterscotch pudding. I asked my husband if we could leave early to buy her some for supper.

As we drove through the parking lot of the food store, I noticed a black limousine and a man in a black tuxedo standing by the door. There was also a white van and some teenagers close by. I thought that there must be a prom somewhere tonight.

We drove up to the store and when I opened the door to get out, a boy and a girl about 15 years old were there. The girl handed me a turkey and I said to her, "Why me?" She said, "Because God loves you."

I saw the limousine and the van back out of the parking lot in the mirror. This all happened so fast. I was sitting there holding a turkey and no space to put it in my freezer. We drove to my daughter's house in a city nearby and gave it to her. My mother did not get any pudding that night, but God had answered my repeated prayer, Lord,

fill my cup and let it run over that others would have. My daughter and I both had turkeys as a result of God answering my prayer, confirming most of all that God loved me. He had gone out of his way to show it!

*And it shall come to pass in the last days, saith God, I will pour out of my Spirit upon all flesh: and your sons and your daughters shall prophesy, and your young men shall see visions, and your old men shall dream dreams:*
*Acts 2:17*

# Dream Revealing to me
# my Mother's Death

Before my mother's death, the Lord showed me in a dream that she was going to die. In the dream, I saw men carrying my mother's coffin up the railroad to the graveyard where she was to be buried. I believe He allowed me to see this for two purposes, for her awareness and to prepare me for this great loss.

Two weeks later, my mom became ill and was taken by ambulance from the nursing home to the emergency room. After spending all day there, she was admitted to the hospital. Many family members came to visit her. I stayed with her during the night and also shared with others what I had seen in the dream. It was then I realized that my mom did not know and I told her during the night that this time she was not going to get better, but was going to heaven and that one day I would come and be with her. She did not say anything but squeezed my hand with the knowledge that she understood. She was in the hospital several days and then was taken back to the nursing home, where she died. Her room

was filled with her children, grandchildren and others as she left this world. I clung to her, not able to say goodbye. Then finally I released her, as her spirit had already departed.

# The Unseen Angel

My mother died in December of 2005. I was deeply mourning her passing as I was very close to her several years before her death.

About two weeks after her passing, I was sitting on the back pew of our church during the worship service and someone touched me on the right shoulder. I felt energy go through my body, but no one was there. From that moment, my heart was healed of the loss of my mother and I rejoice, believing that I will be with her in heaven.

*Matthew 5:4*
*Blessed are they that mourn: for they shall be comforted.*

# This Too Shall Pass

In August 2009, around 6 p.m., my husband was using the ladder to remove a cable from the roof when the ladder slipped and he fell, breaking both bones in one leg above the ankle and several bones in his left foot. After surgery and spending many weeks at the Veterans Administration Hospital, he came home. He was in a wheelchair and used a board to slide from the bed to the chair. I was his caregiver and I was exhausted. He began to run a fever and vomited about suppertime one night. He was very sick. I called my sister to come and help me take him to the emergency room at the V.A. She came and we got him into the car. I rode in the back seat and was so worn out, feeling I could do nothing more. As we were going down Roan Street in Johnson City, TN, the Lord spoke in my left ear, "This too shall pass." Immediately, I was refreshed and was able to do what I had to do. They kept my husband overnight at the hospital because he had an infection.

# Reassuring Dream about my First Hip Replacement

For many years I had suffered with pain in my back and legs. The pain became worse as I became older. I had been given several epidurals, which helped for a while, but then became useless. Eventually, I was referred to a surgeon, who took x-rays and told me I needed a hip replacement as the pain was coming from bone rubbing against bone of the hip joints.

I was not too happy to be told this and unsure of my future, even if I would live during the surgery because I was worn out with much suffering.

I sought God about the replacement of the hip and my recovery. He answered by showing me a dream. In the dream, I was running in a race on the street where I live and then I was leaping. This encouraged me so much, because I knew I was going to live and become well again. I had the surgery and recovered with no pain in that joint.

# Dream about Second Hip Replacement

After the first hip replacement, I was told that my other hip was as bad as the first one had been or worse, and it would have to be replaced. I was more inclined to have this surgery, but still uncertain about my future. I sought the Lord about this hip replacement and he again answered me in a dream.

I dreamed that my husband and I were looking at a house. Each room was beautiful. When we went downstairs, there was a room that was not finished. In the dream, I felt like this was my house. I understood by the dream that my life was not over and that I still had work to do; my building was not complete yet. I had the surgery and am recovering well at the writing of this book. Thanks be to God, who loves us and wants to communicate with us.

# Road Sign

In the past I wrote a small book, giving my testimony about searching for God and receiving salvation. After both of my hip replacement surgeries, I gave this book to all who were taking care of me and talked about the Lord to anyone who would listen.

One night after my second hip replacement while recovering at the rehabilitation facility, I dreamed that I was a road sign at a cross roads with an arrow showing the way to go.

I felt very humbled after this dream. As I am almost well from both surgeries, I look forward to the future with the desire to fulfill my destiny, the calling of my Lord Jesus Christ.

# Whosoever Will

*And the Spirit and the bride say, Come. And let him that heareth say, Come. And let him that is athirst come. And whosoever will, let him take the water of life freely.*
*Revelation 22:17*

# About the Author

Shirley Ferguson currently resides in Northeast, Tennessee. As a young woman, she studied to be a nurse and worked on and off throughout the years in this profession. She has spent her life caring for others and teaching them about the Lord. She is a licensed and ordained minister and is a member of a church in Southwest, Virginia. Shirley is driven with a passion to create and sew, enjoying and producing many quilts, articles of clothing, and crafts for herself and others.

Her desire is that you will use the experiences she has shared with you in this book to ensure that you are ready to meet the Lord, and that you will have a closer walk with Him.